Key Stage 2

English
Practice Test Booklet

Author
Jeff Hale

EDUCATIONAL

The Author and Publisher are grateful to the following for permission to reproduce copyright materials: © Charles Causley, from the anthology *The Possum Tree* edited by Lesley Pyott, permission kindly granted by David Higham Associates Ltd.; © R Chetwynd-Hayes from the anthology *Ghost after Ghost*, Penguin UK; © Catherine Storr from the story 'Christmas in the Rectory' from the anthology *Ghost after Ghost*, Penguin UK; © Angela Grunsell taken from *Let's Talk About – Stepfamilies*, Alladin Books Ltd.; © Jan Mark 1985, from *Trouble Half Way*, published by Viking Kestrel and reproduced by permission of Penguin UK.

Every effort has been made to trace copyright holders and to obtain their permission for the use of copyright material. The authors and publishers will gladly receive information enabling them to rectify any error or omission in subsequent editions.

First published 1996
New editions 1997, 1998
This edition 1999
Reprinted 2000

Letts Educational, 9–15 Aldine Street, London W12 8AW
Tel. 020 8740 2266
Fax 020 8743 8451
E-mail:mail@lettsed.co.uk

Text © Letts Educational Ltd 1996, 1997, 1998, 1999
Author: Jeff Hale

Editorial, design and production by Hart McLeod, Cambridge
and adapted by Ken Vail Graphic Design, Cambridge

British Library Cataloguing-in-Publication Data
A CIP record for this book is available from the British Library

ISBN 1 84085 328 X

Printed in Great Britain by Ashford Colour Press

English

Reading Comprehension
Test A Levels 3–5

First Name:

Last Name:

School:

General Instructions

Read all the words carefully including the special instructions on page 4.

The questions for you to answer are in grey boxes.

For example:

What does the writer mean . . . .?

Look for the ✐ to show you where to write your answer.

Remember to explain your answers by referring to the passage in your reading booklet if you are asked to do so.

GOOD LUCK!

Instructions

Questions and Answers

In this booklet there are different types of questions for you to answer in different ways. The space for your answer shows you what type of writing is needed. Answer each question by referring to the extract from the story you have been given. The tests include questions expecting:

- **short line answers**
  Some questions are followed by a short line. This shows that you need only write a word or phrase in your answer.

- **several line answers**
  Some questions are followed by a few lines. This gives you space to write more words or a sentence or two.

- **multiple-choice answers**
  On some pages there are some questions where you need do no writing at all. You need to choose the best word or group of words to answer the question and put a ring around your choice.

Here is an example of this type of question.

The title of the story is:

 Dead Ghost   The Brown Bear   The Great Escape

The marks in boxes tell you how many marks there are for each question.

When working through the questions, you can refer back to the story at any time.

The questions in this section are about the poem *Colonel Fazackerley* by Charles Causley.

Read the poem *Colonel Fazackerley* on page 1 of your reading booklet.

Answer all the questions.

1 **In the first verse of this poem, how is the castle described?**

_____

| 1 |

2 **In the second verse, the writer says that the ghost 'shivered, beware'. Why does the writer describe the ghost as shivering? Is it because:**

   a   the ghost is cold?
   b   the ghost is frightening?
   c   the ghost's image is flickering and hard to see?

_____

| 1 |

3 **Look at the first four verses.
List <u>three</u> other descriptions of the ghost given in these verses.**

   1 _____

   2 _____

   3 _____

| 3 |

4 List <u>three</u> ways that the ghost tries to frighten the Colonel in the last **five** verses.

1 _____

2 _____

3 _____

3

5 Is the poem meant to be frightening or funny? Give an example of a line from the poem to support your answer.

_____

_____

2

6 Towards the end of the poem (verse 8), the writer says 'the ghost vanished, his efforts in vain'.

a   What were these efforts?
b   Why were they in vain?

a _____

_____

b _____

2

_____

The questions in this section are about the story *Dead Ghost* by R. Chetwynd-Hayes.

Read the story *Dead Ghost* on pages 2–7 of your reading booklet.

Answer all the questions.

Section I

1 **How do we know it was a hot day? Put a ring around the correct answer. Is it because the writer says:**

| there was no breeze | a heat haze rose from the meadows |

1

2 **Why is the river described as 'wending its way between the banks'? Put a ring around the correct answer. Is it because:**

| the river is full of weeds | the water was moving quickly | the water is not moving at all | the river runs through a series of bends |

1

3 **List <u>two</u> phrases from the first paragraph which suggest that, when we first meet him, Gerald is feeling very calm.**

1 _____

2 _____

2

4 Why did Gerald frown when his sister spoke? Put a ring around the correct answer. Is it because:

| he was thinking of something important | he was asleep | he didn't like his sister | she had interrupted his peaceful and calm mood |

1

5 When Gerald refers to his sister's 'unnatural beauty', is he:

| saying he finds his sister attractive | being a little bit sarcastic |

1

Put a ring around the correct answer.

The following questions ask you for longer written answers. Try to answer them in as much detail as you can.

Section II

6 Why does Gerald tell Catherine to stop pretending?

_____

_____

_____

7 How does Catherine first describe the appearance of the woman she thinks she has seen?

_____

_____

8 What effect does this description of the woman immediately have on Gerald?

_____

9 Suggest <u>two</u> clues given by the writer that let us know that Catherine is becoming more and more anxious.

1 _____

_____

2 _____

_____

10 Give <u>two</u> examples of something that the writer says to suggest that Gerald is now also becoming anxious.

1 _____

2 _____

_____

11 Why does the writer say the house 'seemed to smile'?

_____

_____

_____

12 When Gerald and Catherine return home, the writer suggests that the house is rather large. Give <u>two</u> examples of words he uses to do this.

1 _____

2 _____

13 Catherine says to Gerald, 'You won't tell Mother or Father about this, will you?'. What is it that she wants to be kept secret?

_____

_____

_____

3

14 When Gerald and Catherine first meet Mr Makepeace, he 'frowns with disapproval'. What has upset him?

1 _____

2 _____

2

15 Give <u>one</u> example of an important difference in the physical appearance between Mr and Mrs Makepeace.

_____

_____

1

16 Suggest <u>three</u> possible reasons why Mrs Makepeace interrupts her husband.

1 _____

2 _____

3 _____

3

Letts

17 The writer describes Gerald as 'alarmed' by his sister's question about the age of the house. What exactly is it that has alarmed him?

_____

_____

_____

18 Who responds first to Mr Makepeace's criticism of the Earl? What does he or she say?

1 _____

_____

2 _____

_____

19 What two things does Mr Makepeace say that reveal his opinion of the vicar?

1 _____

_____

2 _____

_____

20 What does Mr Makepeace want Gerald to do?
Does the writer think Gerald will succeed?
Give a reason for your answer based on what you have read in the passage.

1 _____

2 _____

3 _____

_____

Letts

English

Writing Test A Levels 3–5

Time 45 minutes
plus 15 minutes planning time

First Name:

_____

Last Name:

_____

School:

_____

Instructions

In this booklet you will find four different topics that you could write about.

You should choose **ONE only**.
Read the booklet carefully and choose a topic.

 Tick the title you have chosen.

Either: Story Writing
☐ "But you promised!"

☐ The Great Inventor

☐ Simply the best

Or: Information Writing
☐ Making television programmes more interesting

 Below each title you will find a list of ideas to think about. Use these ideas only if you think they are helpful.

Inside this booklet you will also find a **planning sheet.** This is to help you to make notes so that you can plan your ideas **before** you start to write your story or article.

Use the next 15 minutes to plan your writing.

Your teacher will then give you another booklet for you to write in full what you want to say.

You have 45 minutes to finish your writing.

Story Writing

If you have decided to choose the story writing option, you will have chosen topic 1, 2 or 3. The ideas below may be of help but you may prefer to use your own ideas. Use the planning sheet to jot down some ideas.

1 **"But you promised!"**

"But you promised", howled Jenny in despair. "I wouldn't have offered in the first place, if you hadn't said it was OK!"

"Well, I can't help all that", said her mother, crossly. "You'll just have to cancel it. I told you weeks ago that you couldn't do it."

Write a short story using this opening to help you.

You should think about:

- who is involved in the story

 What have the people in your story been discussing?
Why will it have to be cancelled?
What will each character say next? How will this conversation develop?

- what the characters are like

 What words will you use to describe them?
How do they behave and what does this tell us about them?
What might they be thinking about?
How do they treat each other?

- what happens as the story unfolds

 What happens next? Will the event really be cancelled? Who will get her way? What else will happen as the story develops?
Who else might be involved in the story? How will you introduce them? What will they do or say? How will the story finish?

2 The Great Inventor

Write a short story about someone who has invented something very important.

You should think about:

- the characters and setting for your story

 Is the inventor a real person or someone you have made up?
What makes the invention great?
What events will your account or story describe?
When will it be set? Now? Long ago? In the future?
What are the characters and the setting of your story like?
If the story has action, where will it take place?
What do the people do? What are they like? What do they say?

- the language and ideas used in the story

 How will you introduce your ideas?
Will you just write a simple story or will you show that you approve or are critical of what happened? How will you do this?
Will you use paragraphs? If so, what ideas will they discuss or describe? Will you include dialogue?
How will you link your ideas? How will you build up to a conclusion?

3 **Simply the best**

Write a short story using the title to guide you.

You should think about:

- the main events that occur in your story

 Who or what is it that is 'the best' – is it a meal, a prize, a holiday, a person, something quite different?
Why are they the best? What do they do? What do they look like?
What happens as the story develops?
How will your story end?

- the characters and setting for your story

 What are the characters in your story like?
Where does the action take place? What is it like?
What do the people do? What do they say?

- the language you might use

 Will you use lots of adjectives/describing words?

Think about linking your ideas with words such as 'while', 'however', 'meanwhile', 'yet'.

Will you use conversation? What people say, and how they say it, are good ways of telling your reader what they are like. It also helps to keep the story going. If you do, remember to set it out clearly, using speech marks and other punctuation accurately.

Information writing

If you have decided to do the information writing option, this is your topic. The ideas below may be of help but you may use ideas of your own if you prefer. Use the planning sheet to jot down some ideas.

4 **Making television programmes more interesting**

Imagine that you have been asked, as part of your classwork, to:

a carry out some research into what kinds of television programmes people like best
b describe how, if given the chance, you would go about making programmes more interesting.

You have been told that you will then be asked either to give a talk on what you found out to the rest of your class, or to write an article.

You should think about:

In your First Section

• Describe how you will set about researching people's favourite programmes.

For example, you might think about some of the points below:

Who will you ask?
Where will you meet them?
What kinds of questions will you ask?
Would you, or anyone helping you, need advice on how to approach people, particularly strangers?
How will you set your questions out?

How will you set your results out? Will you write a simple discussion or will you set the information out in any particular way, perhaps in table form? If so, say why this will help you get your ideas across better.

In your Second Section

- Describe your own preferences and explain why your chosen programmes are better than those being shown at present.

 As you do this, remember that you will be trying to *persuade other people in your class* that your views are justified.
How will you set about doing this?
What kind of language or presentation method will you use?
Could you perhaps include graphs and a commentary?
How might this help?

Writing Planning sheet

Use this page to jot down ideas for your story, presentation or article. **Your notes will not be marked.**

English

Spelling and Handwriting Test A
Levels 3–5   *Ghost After Ghost*

Time 45 minutes (30 minutes for spelling)

First Name:

_____

Last Name:

_____

School:

_____

Instructions

Spelling Test

Your teacher is going to read a short test passage to you. It comes from the story *Ghost After Ghost* edited by Aidan Chambers.

It will contain words which are missing from your test paper.

When your teacher comes to these words he or she will stop reading for a moment.

You should then write the missing words in the spaces.

You will get one mark for each word that is spelt correctly.

Handwriting Test

The test asks you to copy out the short passage taken from the same story *Ghost After Ghost.*

You should write the passage very neatly in the space provided.

Remember to do your best handwriting, joining the letters if you can.

Spelling Test A

Listen to the story.
Write the missing words in the spaces.
Spell the words correctly.

Both of the _____ sisters slept _____ that night, a

heavy _____ sleep from which they woke with

_____ . But in the _____ of the next morning, Kate

began to believe that she must have been _____ from

_____ the night before. Fanny _____ less

_____ , and Steven, full of triumph and _____

carefree, led his aunts off to visit his _____ , to watch

him trying to make a great crab _____ out from

_____ its protective overhang of rock, and to show how

well he could negotiate the long _____ of spiked rocks

which ran out into the _____ . The only _____

was that there was still no wind. The sea lay smooth and

white under the overcast sky, and the shore was silent

_____ for the _____ and the suck of the water

where it met the sand, like the _____ of a conspiracy, a

secret not to be _____ .

20

Letts

Here is a short extract from the book of ghost stories
Ghost After Ghost edited by Aidan Chalmers.

**Write it out very neatly in your own handwriting.
You will be given a mark for your handwriting.
Remember to make your handwriting as neat as
possible, joining your letters if you can.**

In the afternoon, William walked
the sisters to the village, a huddle
of cottages and an inn near the
squat grey tower of the church.
There wasn't much to admire in
the building and Kate and Susan
walked around the outside.

5

English

Reading Comprehension
Test B   Levels 3–5

First Name:

_____

Last Name:

_____

School:

_____

General Instructions

Read all the words carefully including the special instructions on page 26.

The questions for you to answer are in grey boxes.

For example:

What does the writer mean. . . . . . .?

Look for the ✎ to show you where to write your answer.

Remember to explain your answers by referring to the passage in your reading booklet if you are asked to do so.

GOOD LUCK!

Instructions

Questions and Answers

In this booklet there are different types of questions for you to answer in different ways. The space for your answer shows you what type of writing is needed. Answer each question by referring to the extract from the story you have been given. The test includes questions expecting:

- **short line answers**
  Some questions are followed by a short line. This shows that you need only write a word or phrase in your answer.

- **several line answers**
  Some questions are followed by a few lines. This gives you space to write more words or a sentence or two.

- **multiple-choice answers**
  On some pages there are some questions where you need do no writing at all. You need to choose the best word or group of words to answer the question and put a ring around your choice.

  Here is an example of this type of question:

The marks in boxes tell you how many marks there are for each question.

When working through the question, you can refer back to the story at any time.

The questions in this section are about the book *Stepfamilies* by A. Grunsell.

Read the story *Stepfamilies* on pages 8–9 of your reading booklet.

Answer all the questions.

Section I

1 **List <u>four</u> different ways in which the extract says a stepfamily can come about.**

1 _____

2 _____

3 _____

4 _____   **4**

2 **What <u>two</u> things does the extract say people in every kind of family always need?**

1 _____

2 _____   **2**

3 **When Georgio and his father were talking, Georgio's stepmother found it hard to say something. What was this?**

1 _____   **1**

4   What <u>two</u> things did the members of Georgio's family do to overcome this difficulty?

1 _____

2 _____

5   The writer says that stepparents and their children don't have to love each other. People will react differently. Give <u>two</u> examples mentioned in the passage showing how they react.

1 _____

2 _____

The questions in this section are about the story *Trouble Half-Way* by Jan Mark

Read the story *Touble Half-Way* on pages 10–14 of your reading booklet.

Answer all the questions.

Section II

1 **How does the writer describe what it was like to move around the house? Put a ring around the correct answer. Was it:**

| really difficult to see | dark and spooky | like a playground game | freezing cold |

| **1** |

2 **The children found it difficult to move around the house. Why was this? Put a ring around the correct answer. Was it:**

| the children didn't like each other | they made too much noise | there were only four of them | they kept meeting each other |

| **1** |

3 Amy describes Richard and Helen as 'plodding' down to the park. Does this mean:

| they walked in a tired way | they kept arguing | they were on Helen's cart | they were running |

1

Put a ring around the correct answer.

4 When Amy and her mother first begin to speak, Amy is in a mood. What kind of mood is it? Is she:

| pleased to be talking to her mum | miserable | keen to help | unsteady |

1

Put a ring around the correct answer.

5 Amy's cloth is described as 'anti-static'. Does this mean it is:

| very clean | very dirty | treated so it won't pick up dust | cheap |

1

Put a ring around the correct answer.

6 Why did Amy jump back when the telephone rang?

_____

_____

2

7 Why does the writer describe Gran's voice as 'unexpectedly sharp'?

1 _____

_____

2 _____

_____

3 _____

3

8 Amy says there is one person that 'she had never quite forgiven' for knowing about Richard. Who is she referring to?

_____

1

9 What does the writer mean when she says that Mrs Varley will be able to 'cushion the impact'?

1 _____

2 _____

_____

2

10 Give <u>two</u> examples from the passage that describe the way Amy feels when she is described as 'flapping her hands'.

1 _____

2 _____

2

11 What does Mrs Varley mean when she says "You're always meeting trouble half-way, you and your mum"?

_____

_____

2

12 Give <u>two</u> reasons why Amy thinks that 55 is 'old enough to be dead'?

1 _____

2 _____

2

13 When Amy goes back into the house, she is immediately certain that something is very wrong.

a What is it that tells her this? Explain how you have arrived at your answer by referring to the passage.

_____

_____

b What does the problem turn out to be? Explain how you have arrived at your answers by referring to the passage.

_____

_____

3

14 Richard's family are described by the writer as people Amy knows 'only as smiles in photographs'. Why is this? Give <u>two</u> reasons given in the passage to support your answer.

1 _____

2 _____

2

15 After making a telephone call, Richard says, "I can't go and tell him to shove it all back in, can I?" Who is Richard talking about? How do you know?

_____

_____

_____

2

16 Amy realises that 'there will have to be rearrangements'. What does she mean? Give a reason from the text to support your answer.

_____

_____

2

17 How does Amy feel about this probable change?

_____

_____

_____

18 What kind of person is Richard? Give an example from the passage of something he does to support your answer.

_____

_____

_____

19 Which of the three characters we have met so far seems to you to be most 'in control' of what they are doing? Give reasons from the passage to support your answer.

_____

_____

_____

20 Richard is described as speaking 'tactlessly'. Why?

_____

_____

21 What reasons does Richard give for his view that Amy should stay with him?

1 _____

_____

2 _____

_____

22 Towards the end of the passage Richard is described as 'knowing what Amy is thinking'. We don't know for sure what this is but it could be many things. What do you think Amy might be thinking? Try to justify your answer by referring to the events described in the passage.

_____

_____

_____

English

Writing   Test B   Levels 3–5

Time 45 minutes
plus 15 minutes planning time

First Name:

_____

Last Name:

_____

School:

_____

Instructions

In this booklet you will find four different topics that you could write about.

You should choose **ONE** only.

Read the booklet carefully and choose a topic.

Tick the title you have chosen.

Either: Story Writing
☐ The never-ending sausage

☐ The mountainside

☐ A bad accident

Or: Information Writing
☐ A full eclipse of the sun

Below each title you will find a list of ideas to think about. Use these ideas only if you think they are helpful.

Inside this booklet you will also find a **_planning sheet_**. This is to help you to make notes so that you can plan your ideas **before** you start to write your story or article.

Use the next 15 minutes to plan your writing.

Your teacher will then give you another booklet for you to write in full what you want to say.

You have 45 minutes to finish your writing.

Story Writing

If you have decided to choose the story writing option, you will have chosen topic 1, 2 or 3. The ideas below may be of help but you may prefer to use your own ideas. Use the planning sheet to jot down some ideas.

1 The never-ending sausage

Write a short story using the title to guide you.

You should think about:

- the main events that occur in your story

 Why is the sausage 'never-ending'? How are we first introduced to it?
Where is the story set?

What happens as the story develops? Is the story meant to be funny? What will occur to show this?

How will you link your ideas? Using words or phrases such as 'all of a sudden', 'meanwhile', 'just as...' helps the story to develop. They can also help you create a sense that something dramatic or surprising is going to happen.

Will you use conversation or speech? Conversation is a good way of showing what your characters are like. If you do use conversation, remember to use speech marks and other punctuation accurately.

How will your story end? Is there a special trick or twist to your ending that would make it really interesting or unusual?

- the characters in your story

 What are the characters in your story like?
What do these people do?
What do they say?
How will you describe them and what they do?

- the setting for your story

 Will you use lots of adjectives/describing words to set the scene?
Describing words help the reader to understand what a place is
like. This helps create a good 'atmosphere'. You might even use
complete phrases to get across a particular effect.

2   The mountainside

*The large black bird soared high above the mountain
top and circled lazily, watching the sheep far below.
None of the animals appeared to have any idea of their
danger. The shepherd watched and worried. Soon it
would begin to get dark. What was he to do?*

Write a short story using this opening to help you.

You should think about:

- who is involved in the story

 What is the shepherd worried about?
How has he come to be there?
What might have happened already in the story which you might
need to refer back to?
What other characters will your story contain?
How will you introduce them to the reader?

- what the characters are like

 How will you describe the life of the shepherd?
What kind of person is he? Tough? Not easily surprised? Talkative or uncommunicative? Someone who it is easy to make friends with, or not? Why?
What are the other characters like?

How will you describe the animals' behaviour, and that of the bird, in the period leading up to the action described in your story, as well as afterwards?

- what happens as the story unfolds

 What happens next? How do all the characters in the story react?
What else will happen as the story unfolds?
Why is the fact that it will soon get dark important?

Is your story designed to make the reader feel happy or sad, or some other emotion? What kinds of language will you use to create this effect?

How will the story finish?

3 **A bad accident**

> **Write a short story using the title to guide you.**

You should think about:

- the development of the story (its plot)

 What kind of accident is it? How does it happen?
Is it something you have actually witnessed yourself or is it a fictional event that you are describing?
Where will it take place? Who is affected? Why is it so bad?
If the story has action, where will it take place?
What do the people do? What are they like? What do they say?

- the characters in your story

 If your story has different characters, what are they like? It helps to keep the reader interested if you can make them sound interesting. How will you describe them?

- the language and the ideas used in the story

 Since the account is about a bad accident, how will you make your ideas capture the reader's attention? How will you link your ideas?
You could use words and phrases such as 'While', 'Yet', 'but for all that…' or 'Even as he spoke…' for example. Try to build up to a conclusion so that it develops naturally out of all that has already happened in your story.

How will you set your ideas out? Will you use paragraphs? If so, what ideas will they discuss or describe?

Will you include dialogue? How will you use dialogue to help set the scene you are describing? If you do, remember to use speech marks and other punctuation accurately.

Are there any general lessons you think we should all learn from this accident? How will your account convey these lessons?

Information Writing

If you have decided to do the information writing, this is your topic. The ideas below may be of help but you may use ideas of your own if you prefer. Use the planning sheet to jot down some ideas.

4 A full eclipse of the sun

As you probably know, there was a full eclipse of the sun in August 1999. The best place to see it was in Cornwall.

Imagine that it is the month before the eclipse. You have been asked to write to all your relatives to suggest that you and they should change your holiday plans so that the whole family can go to Cornwall to be present when it occurs. If you saw the eclipse, use your experience to be as persuasive as possible.

Write a letter to one relative:

- explaining what the eclipse will be like
- setting out the reasons why it would be worth everyone making a special effort to be together, even if this meant changing plans of their own
- anticipating some of their objections
- suggesting reasons why they should come anyway, which might convince them.

A full eclipse of the sun *(additional guidance notes)*

Style

The letter you are going to write will have to be persuasive; it will also be addressed to someone you know quite well so it can be fairly familiar or informal in tone. Try to decide how you will express your ideas – will you begin 'Dear Auntie'/'Dear Uncle' and go on to say something like 'Hey, I've had this really great idea...' for example? Or would it be better to begin 'I understand from my mother that you had intended to...'?

Content

You will also need to decide whether to explain what an eclipse is, how much detail to go into and why Cornwall is the best place to view it from. Similarly, you will have to decide how far to 'talk up' the eclipse; will you make it sound exciting, mysterious, frightening – or will you simply stress the advantages of all the family being together on this unique occasion? You could, of course, do both! Try to make your language and descriptions suitable for the purpose you have in mind.

Structure

You will also need to decide how to lay your letter out. Remember! This letter will be to relatives so you probably won't want to include too many paragraphs. But you have to introduce the 'right tone' as described above and you will also have to be 'persuasive' since you are attempting to change other people's holiday plans. This will probably mean that you will need to distinguish these different ideas in your letter.

Finally, you may want to take this opportunity to offer some family news. If so, this will change the theme of the letter and you might need to write this section in a different way. How will you introduce this change of emphasis? You will need to use appropriate phrases to indicate that your letter has now changed its purpose.

Writing Planning sheet

Use this page to jot down your ideas
Your notes will not be marked.

English

Spelling and Handwriting   Test B
Levels 3–5 *Trouble Half-Way*

Time 45 minutes (30 minutes for Spelling)

Name:

_____

Instructions

Spelling Test

- Your teacher is going to read a short test passage to you. It comes from the story *Trouble Half-way.*

- It will contain words which are missing from your test paper.

- When your teacher comes to these words he or she will stop reading for a moment.

- You should then write the missing words in the spaces.

- You will get one mark for each word which is spelt correctly.

Handwriting Test

- The test asks you to copy out a passage taken from the story *Trouble Half-Way*.

- You should write the passage very neatly in the space provided.

- Remember to do your best handwriting, joining the letters if you can.

Listen to the story.
Write the missing words in the spaces.
Spell the words correctly.

She went up to bed at half past nine. _____ , there

was an _____ about this on Saturdays but _____

she went _____ and could not help _____ that

Richard had switched off the television before she

_____ the top of the stairs. She was soon asleep. The

next morning she _____ out of the bathroom window

and saw him clearing a _____ path of earth among the

weeds that Dad would never have allowed to become so

_____ . When he had finished, he moved away and

stood looking at the _____ sections of greenhouse.

Evidently he _____ to spend the day in the garden.

Amy managed to keep herself _____, first tidying up,

then putting in some _____ practice in the living

room with the furniture pushed back, wearing her

_____ leg-warmers. _____, she was aware of a

distant clatter from the garden and when, finally, she came in

to make tea, she saw Richard in the middle of the lawn,

surrounded by _____ of the greenhouse, laid out like

an _____ toy kit. He seemed a little discouraged.

Amy almost felt sorry for him as he stood there, soaked by

the continuing _____, when he could have remained

inside by the fire which she had _____ lit in

the _____ .

Letts

Handwriting Test B

Here is a short passage that continues the story *Trouble Half-Way* which you have been reading.

Write it out very neatly in your best handwriting. Remember to make your handwriting as neat as possible, joining your letters if you can.

> Richard turned warily at the sound, saw the jar and nodded with enthusiasm. He's overdoing it a bit, Amy thought, as he came in rubbing his hands, until she saw that his fingers were blue with cold. The thought that the house wasn't big enough for both of them flashed across her mind.

_____

_____

_____

_____

_____

_____

_____

5